THIS BOOK IS

. . . .

THE WORLD'S MOST IDIOTIC/SEXY/
UGLY/ROMANTIC/SMELLY/GORGEOUS/
CHARMING/FAT/USELESS/VIRGOAN

YOURS IN DISGUST/LOTS OF LOVE

BEST WISHES . . . .

P.S. PLEASE TAKE NOTE OF PAGE(S)

. . . .

Ian Heath's Virgo Book

ISBN 978-1-905134-08-3

Published by Ian Heath Books
9 Adam Street
The Strand
London WC2N 6AA

www.ianheathart.com

Ian heath's

VIRGO

BOOK

VIRGO

AUGUST 22 – SEPTEMBER 22

SIXTH SIGN OF THE ZODIAC
SYMBOL : THE MAIDEN
RULING PLANET : MERCURY
COLOURS : YELLOW, GREY
GEM : ONYX
NUMBER : FIVE
DAY : WEDNESDAY
METAL : ANTIMONY
FLOWER : LAVENDER

ZZZZZZZZ

The VIRGOAN at work...............

............IS SLOW..................

............HONEST..................

.... CAN BE TOUCHY...............

.....WILL DO ANYTHING.............

.... DRESSES SMARTLY...........

.........IS HARD-HEADED...........

...... DELEGATES WELL..............

...NEVER TIRES OF PUBLIC DUTY......

..... IS SOMETIMES CARELESS...........

.... AND ADVENTUROUS.

..... A DOORMAN ....

..........POPCORN PACKER.............

SECURITY GUARD

.... RESEARCH CHEMIST...........

......TREE-SURGEON.................

......DENTAL MECHANIC...........

..... OR CAR SALESMAN.

.... IS STRICT......................

....LIKES INTELLIGENT FRIENDS....

..... MAKES WINE ....

...... IS AN OBSERVER ....

.....NOT A GOOD LISTENER........

.....A USELESS GARDENER........

...... A DEDICATED COOK............

.... A GOSSIP..................

..... LIKES READING STORIES ....

....AND WON'T PAY BILLS.

.... PRESSED FLOWERS.........

..........FLYING..................

......DISCUSSING POLITICS..........

......HOT, SANDY PLACES...........

.... HOT BATHS................

.... AND CHOCOLATE MOUSSE.

......RECEIVING BILLS......

. . . . LOUD NOISES . . . .

...... MAKING DECISIONS..........

.......TAPIOCA PUDDING.............

...... AND FOOTBALL.

The VIRGOAN in love......................

......ANALYSES PARTNER...........

.....CAN BE JEALOUS.................

.......IS VERY UNSURE...............

....RESISTS SEDUCTIVE ADVANCES....

.....IS VERY SELF-CENTRED............

......PLAYS HARD TO GET............

.... DOES NOT WANT TO DOMINATE ...

.......IS PASSIONATE..............

.... FAITHFUL..................

.... AND POSSESSIVE.

VIRGOAN AND PARTNER

HEART RATINGS

♥♥♥♥♥ WOWEE!!
♥♥♥♥ GREAT, BUT NOT 'IT'
♥♥♥ O.K. — COULD BE FUN
♥♥ FORGET IT
♥ RUN THE OTHER WAY —FAST!

CAPRICORN TAURUS

LIBRA SCORPIO CANCER
LEO

SAGITTARIUS VIRGO

PISCES GEMINI

AQUARIUS ARIES

VIRGO PEOPLE

FREDDIE MERCURY · HUGH GRANT
D H LAWRENCE · BARRY WHITE
AGATHA CHRISTIE · H G WELLS
MICKEY ROURKE · SAM NEILL
KEANU REEVES · PRINCE HARRY

PETER SELLERS · PAULO COELHO
CAMERON DIAZ · BUDDY HOLLY
SEAN CONNERY · GLORIA ESTAFAN
CLAUDIA SCHIFFER · GENE KELLY
ELVIS COSTELLO · JEREMY IRONS
IVAN THE TERRIBLE · B B KING
GLORIA GAYNOR · BEYONCÉ
ROALD DAHL · OTIS REDDING
JOSÉ FELICIANO · SOPHIA LOREN
HARRY CONNICK JR · TWIGGY
CHARLIE SHEEN · RACHEL WARD